Why Creeps Don't Know They're Creeps

**What Game of Thrones can teach us
about relationships and Hollywood scandals**

A brief commentary on the recent high profile
sex scandals in Hollywood and Washington D.C.
by Oliver Markus Malloy

Becker and Malloy
www.beckerandmalloy.com

Table of Contents

INTRODUCTION

This book deals with highly sensitive subject matter.

It is not an attempt to make excuses for sexual predators. It is an attempt to prevent sexual misconduct in the future, by examining the chain of events, and misunderstandings along the way, that lead to sexual misconduct.

We can't fix a problem if we don't understand the problem or don't even know why there is a problem in the first place.

In my previous book, *Why Men And Women Can't Be Friends*, I talked about how men and women often fundamentally misunderstand each other without even realizing it.

Sometimes both sides completely misread the other person's social cues. Men and women often perceive the same situation very differently.

For example, studies have shown that women tend to misinterpret a man's sexual interest in her as "just being friendly" and men tend to misinterpret a woman's friendliness as sexual interest in him.

I'M NOT A RACIST, BUT...

When someone starts a sentence like that, the odds are pretty good that what they're about to say next is racist.

Most racists nowadays aren't openly racist like those Alt-Right idiots who march around with torches and shout dumb racial slurs.

Most racists nowadays don't even know they're racist. They might even tell everyone how *not* racist they are. But then they unwittingly repeat and agree with disguised racist propaganda like: "Black people will never learn how to stand on their own two feet if we as a society keep helping them."

And then these unaware racists honestly think they're doing the right thing by supporting a politician who cuts healthcare or school lunch programs in a poor minority neighborhood.

There's a good book about this topic, called *Racism Without Racists*. Basically there are those racists who know they're racists, and then there are racists who have no clue that they're being racist.

The same applies to sexism. Some people don't even know they're sexist. When your old gray-haired boss tells you that "you're pretty good with a computer for a woman," he may very well think he just said something nice to you.

He thinks he did everything right: Don't mention her ass.

Check! Don't mention her tits. Check! Say something nice about her work. Check! So from his perspective, he thinks he should get a gold star for being an exemplary boss, and he has no idea that you're pissed at him or why. Some sexists know they're sexist. Others honestly *don't* know they're sexist.

Take my father for example. He's in his seventies. He is the kindest, sweetest man I know, and he is very respectful towards women. And he adores my mother. He loves her to death. And he has no idea how much it annoys her when they're driving and he talks about how women can't drive. He always makes these comments that women drivers are terrible, and he sees nothing wrong with it, because from his point of view, he thinks he's simply making a factual statement.

He doesn't know that according to insurance company statistics, women are better drivers. Men are more aggressive behind the wheel. Women are safer drivers. That's why insurance premiums for female drivers are lower than for male drivers. Female drivers get into less accidents than men do. They're a lower risk for the insurance company.

So even well-intentioned men can be sexist without realizing it, just as women can be sexist without realizing it.

And, as weird as it sounds, many men don't know when they're acting like sexual predators.

"How can that be?" you might ask. "How could a rapist not

know he's raping someone?"

DICK PICS ANYONE?

Has some guy ever sent you a dick pic out of the blue? Probably. Men love to show their junk to women. And most of them have no idea how creepy that is from your perspective.

Facebook has this feature where you can ask a short question with a colorful background. People go nuts with it and ask all sorts of weird questions, to get as many likes and comments as possible.

Occasionally this question gets asked: "Ladies, do you masturbate to dick pics?"

The men asking that on their Facebook pages think that's a sexy question. They think it will get women to talk about how much they love sex and then they'll want to fuck him for asking such an amazing question. Ahh, romance is alive and well!

These men are genuinely shocked and surprised when a bunch of women reply: "No, I don't. Dick pics are gross and they do nothing for me."

Many men are caught totally off guard by that response, and might even assume that she's just saying that because she's a prude, and afraid she'll look like a slut if she admits how much she loves to get random dick pics and flick the bean.

Men *looove* pussy. They can never get enough of it. If you

send a guy a pussy pic, he's gonna think you're awesome. And he assumes you feel the same way if he sends you an unsolicited dick pic. He loves jerking off while looking at pussy, and in his mind he's certain that you must love dick pics as much as he loves pussy pics. It is such a given to him, it never even occurred to him that it might not be true.

If you have a dog, you know what I'm talking about. Sometimes a dog brings you his favorite toy in the whole world. And he puts it in your lap. Not because he wants you to throw it. This is not for him. This is for you. He wants *you* to have it.

When you look at his toy, all you see is a dirty old sock, covered in crusty dried dog spit. But that's not what he sees. To him that sock is the most awesome thing in the whole world. And he is putting *The Most Awesome Thing In The Whole World* in your lap. Then he sits down in front of you and stares into your eyes as if to say: "This is my gift to you. May it give you the same endless hours of joy and happiness that it has given me."

And that's exactly what men think when they send you a dick pic.

A lot of women are ashamed of their pussies. They think it's not pretty enough. Not the right color. Or the lips are too big or two small. Let me put your fears to rest: There is no such thing as an ugly pussy.

Some women hate their own pussy so much, they can't even stand to look at it. It can be difficult for them to understand that what they see in the mirror is not what men see when they look at it.

You might think your pussy is the wrong color or the wrong shape or the wrong size, but when a man looks at it, all he sees is heaven. Trust me, he's not worried about whether your lips are symmetrical. He's just counting his lucky stars to see you naked. It's very difficult for a man to understand why a woman would be so self-conscious about her hooha.

When a guy jerks off and looks at his dick, he likes what he sees. He thinks: "I have a nice dick!" And he just assumes that of course every woman on the planet would love to see his mighty anaconda.

SOME THINGS CHANGE. SOME DON'T.

A lot of the things we find offensive today weren't always offensive.

For example, in the ancient world, slavery, rape, child marriage, polygamy, and even incest were normal.

In the past, people didn't live as long as we do today, so kids as young as 12 were considered adults, ready to have kids of their own. In many parts of the world, young girls are still being married off at a very young age, and it's normal in their culture to this day.

And George R.R. Martin didn't invent incest when he wrote about the Lannisters in Songs of Ice and Fire (aka Game of Thrones.) He found plenty of real life inspiration in history books.

In ancient Rome incest was pretty common. In ancient Egypt incest was a normal way to keep the royal bloodline pure. Cleopatra was married to her brother, which was perfectly normal back then. Nobody thought they were freaks.

Incest continued throughout the Middle Ages in Europe. The Royals didn't want to taint their blue blood with the blood of commoners.

And incest was still pretty common even as recently as the early days of America. That's why we still joke about rednecks in the south marrying their cousins. (We kid! We kid!) It was normal back then, because frontier towns were pretty small, so you didn't have a lot of dating options. There was no Tinder. A lot of times these settlers only had two choices: Be celibate for the rest of your life or have sex with a relative.

Incest is one of the greatest taboos in our society today. And yet, secretly it still seems to be very popular. People are fascinated by the incestuous relationships on Game of Thrones.

But it doesn't end there.

PornHub is one of the biggest porn sites on the web, with hundreds of millions of users. Everybody loves porn! *Woohoo!*

From time to time they release statistical information about their users. Their year-end stats for 2016 featured a Top 100 list of the most searched porn keywords.

On #5 was... "step sister." *Eeeewww!!!*

And on #2 was... Drum roll please... "step mom!"

That's pretty fucking sick.

So hundreds of millions of people out there like to watch porn that involves having sex with a step sister or a step mother. And I have a feeling that the only reason why there is a "step" at the beginning of those is because actual incest is illegal, so the porn producers get around it by making the actresses pretend they're only "*step* mothers" and "*step* sisters." (Who are you trying to fool? You're only hurting yourself. I'm not mad at you. I'm just disappointed.)

And when you google "step brother romance" on Amazon, you find over 7,400 books featuring lurid tales of imaginary incest, geared towards female readers.

What does it say about our society today if incest is that popular?

We're all a bunch of sick sick puppies. That's what.

When it comes to sexual depravity, we're all guilty of some strange kink or another. Don't tell me you've never fantasized about eating a warm chocolate weed brownie, fresh out of the oven, topped with cherries and vanilla ice cream, while watching porn, having a nice weed buzz, and getting a slow, tender blowjob. Getting all your senses stimulated at the same time! Enjoying every hedonistic earthly sinful pleasure all at once! The Unholy Trifecta!

Or is that just me? Don't lie! Would you want your mom to see what sick barnyard animal creampie porn you googled yesterday? Or what kind of smutty romance you hide on your Kindle?

Didn't think so.

THE WEB BRINGS OUT THE WORST IN PEOPLE

Sometimes, just for fun, I type some random, silly word in front of the word porn and google it. Just to see if it exists. Because that means people out there are getting off on it. So I googled *Nazi porn*. Yupp. It exists. Then I googled *goldfish porn*. Yupp. Found it. Someone out there finds sex with goldfish arousing. *Fart porn*. Yes, that's a thing too, and it brings someone somewhere great pleasure. *Stormtrooper porn*. Yes, the force is strong with that one. And it's not even a Saturday Night Live parody. It's literally hardcore porn, featuring men dressed in Stormtrooper outfits. With surprisingly high production values.

I dare you to find something of which there is no porn.

It would appear that a lot of people out there are hiding their own dark, socially unacceptable sexual fantasies behind a facade of fake indignant outrage when someone else gets caught with their pants down.

Right now we live in an age of extreme Political Correctness. It has gone way too far. I hope it's just a phase. Political Correctness is now just a fancy word for censorship. It's no longer about protecting the weak. It has become an excuse to persecute others, because persecuting people is fun. Don't you dare say or think the wrong thing, or a Twitter mob of angry villagers will come after you with digital torches and metaphorical pitchforks.

No matter what you do, no matter what you say, someone out there will proclaim how outraged they are, because they think it's their job to be offended by every God damn thing. It makes people feel important. It makes them feel powerful. It makes them feel like their opinion is relevant. It's the Yelp effect. Every halfwit who eats food suddenly thinks he's a food critic. And don't get me started on people "reviewing" books they didn't even read. Who needs information, when you can have an uninformed opinion?

Plus, claiming to be offended is a great way to elevate yourself at the expense of others: "Look at me! I'm a much better person than you! And I judge you! I condemn you! Shame! Shame! SHAME!"

These social media shamings bear an uncanny resemblance to medieval witch hunts.

A few years ago I went to the witch museum in Salem, Massachusetts. I never really knew what exactly had happened during the witch hysteria. Yeah, I knew that a mob of overzealous self-righteous villagers killed a bunch of innocent women, but I didn't really know how things could get that far.

Basically, there were these three girls, aged 9 to 11. They were spoiled little brats who misbehaved and had temper tantrums. When they finally got in trouble, as kids often do when they act like little shits, the girls claimed their tantrums weren't really their fault. They blamed the nanny - a black slave. They said the nanny was a witch and she had cast a spell on the girls, and now they were possessed by the devil, and that's why they were acting like typical snot-nosed little teenagers. Sounds about right.

If you were accused of being a witch back then, you were shit out of luck. Being accused was all it took. Forget "innocent until proven guilty." Nobody bothered to prove your guilt. Nobody dared to speak up on your behalf, for fear of being called a witch sympathizer. Because if you were seen as the friend of a witch, you were the next one to be accused of being a witch.

As soon as a woman was accused of being a witch, she was a pariah without any friends. Nobody wanted to be seen in public with her. The whole village ganged up on her. Everyone was trying to outdo everyone else in their anti-witch fervor: "Look at me! I'm throwing rocks at the witch! Look at how much I hate witches! I am definitely NOT a witch myself!"

And if you didn't like your neighbor, because her donkey kept shitting on your front lawn, you just had to accuse her of being a witch to make her disappear. Problem solved.

Whenever I see a social media mob ganging up on a celebrity for supposedly saying something "offensive" it reminds me of the Salem witch hysteria: "That's racist! And me calling you a racist proves that I'm definitely not a racist myself! That's sexist! I shame you! And that means I'm definitely not sexist myself! I shame you for being a bad person. That means I'm a good person! Look at how really really offended I am! That means I'm a really really good person!"

According to the bible, Jesus said "let he who is without sin throw the first rock." But a lot of people seem to think he said: "If you throw rocks at someone else, it proves that you're without sin."

Larry David, the famous Jewish comedian, was on Saturday Night Live and made a Holocaust joke. Some people, non-Jews, claimed to be highly offended on behalf of Jews. Wrap your head around that one. Jews themselves weren't offended by the joke, because Jews tend to have a great sense of humor. You have to, if you have to deal with as much shit as they've had to deal with throughout history. But a bunch of non-Jews claimed to be offended by the joke, calling it racist. That's just absurd. And next thing you know, Larry David is the target of a social media mob. Suddenly a bunch of non-Jews are persecuting a Jew for being Jewish. And they don't see the irony in that.

Political Correctness started out as a movement that intended to protect minorities from harassment. But it has morphed into an excuse for self-righteous zealots to harass people who supposedly offended minorities, even if the minorities don't actually feel offended.

I mean, does any Eskimo *really* feel offended by the word Eskimo? Or have some Political Correctness zealots simply taken it upon themselves to decide for the Eskimos that they should feel offended by that word?

My wife is Asian. She has no idea why she's supposed to be offended by the word Oriental. Who the hell decided that? All this renaming of stuff is just ridiculous. It's just a way for some people to feel powerful and relevant, by telling everyone else what they can and cannot say.

Whenever I see a Political Correctness zealot foaming at the mouth on social media, eager to proclaim how offended they are at every little shit, and using that as an excuse to attack someone for saying or thinking the wrong thing, it reminds me of Cersei Lannister's Walk of Shame on Game of Thrones.

Did you see how spiteful the crowd was? They loved to tear her down. "Well, the villagers didn't like Cersei for what she did," you might think. Sure, that played a role too. But there was something else in their faces: Hateful joy. They *enjoyed* spitting in her face, kicking her, and throwing feces at her naked body.

WHY DO PEOPLE ENJOY TORTURING OTHERS?

I'm a bit of a history nerd. I like reading about how people lived in the past, and I enjoy museums. I've been to a couple of torture museums. It fascinates me how horrible and violent people acted, while believing that *they* were the *good* guys.

In the past, if you were accused (not proven guilty) of witchcraft, blasphemy, heresy or any number of ridiculous accusations, you could be violently tortured.

All these self-righteous zealots back then invented insanely cruel machines to "punish" those who dared to step out of line by being themselves. The herd has a tendency to punish the individualist for being out of step with the herd. Galileo Galilei was punished for saying that the Earth is round, not flat. And not the center of the universe, but circling around the sun. He was right, but it didn't matter. He said something that went against what was commonly believed, so the herd felt the need to punish him for it.

You might think that it was just the establishment, just the king, or just the church, that punished peasants if they dared to speak their own mind. But that's not true. Even the peasants themselves took delight in torturing other peasants, their friends and family, for any arbitrary reason.

One common torture instrument you find in museums is a wooden collar. It's a huge piece of wood with a big hole in the middle. The "sinner" had to stick her head through it and wear the heavy wooden board around her neck. Her hands were often chained to the board as well. Men used to love to do that to their wives, if their wives dared to disobey their husband, or talk back to him. That's right... say the wrong thing and you get tortured. That's all it took. One wrong word. Nothing much has changed today. Forget Free Speech. Use the wrong word, and a mob is eager to torture you for "offending" them. In the eyes of the politically correct Purity Police, being "offensive" is a crime, similar to being a blasphemer.

Here's the real kicker: You'd think that back then the other women (or other husbands) would have done something to stop this cruelty. But no, the opposite happened. The entire village joyfully gathered in the town square and watched as the husband tormented his wife in public. The entire village joined in, kicked her, spat at her, cursed her out, threw rocks and feces at her. The whole community joined in in the torture of one of their own.

That's how people are. The only thing that has changed is that now instead of rocks, the mob uses social media attacks. It doesn't even matter if what you said was really wrong, blasphemous, heretic, racist, sexist or whatever. Mobs become bullies, and bullies don't care whether they're morally right or wrong.

Back then they didn't have TV or the NFL, so watching someone get tortured in the town square was a form of entertainment. And everyone in town joined in. Why? Because everyone else was doing it. You didn't want to be the odd man out, or you'd be the next victim. You had to make sure the other villagers saw you throwing rocks and shit, so you were seen as one of "the good people" not a friend of the victim.

Humans are social animals. Our brains are wired to seek out other humans. Blame evolution. There's safety in numbers. Like many other animals, we feel most comfortable as part of a herd. And when the herd does something, we join in, because we want to be a part of the herd. It literally makes us feel good.

Dopamine is a feel-good chemical our brain releases every time we enjoy something. Medical studies have shown that our brain releases Dopamine when we feel like we're part of a big herd. That explains why the mobs that cheered at Hitler's speeches seemed almost euphoric. It also explains the appeal of cults. It feels good to be surrounded by others who are just like us.

The opposite is also true: Many people feel scared and uncomfortable when they see someone who looks or thinks differently than they do. That's where xenophobia and racism comes from. It's a very old, very primitive instinct. Think about it: why the hell should it matter to you, if someone else looks a little different than you do, or speaks a different language, or thinks a little differently than you do? It really doesn't make a difference in your life, if others are different than you. And yet, somehow we are uncomfortable with it, for no particular reason, other than our old herd instincts.

And when the herd decides to act a certain way, it feels good to do the same thing and be a part of it. You can observe that herd mentality on a daily basis, when you see a group of people (teenagers or biker gangs for example) who all dress alike, even when no one told them how to dress. Or when teenagers all start to use the same slang, because the rest of their little herd does it, so they do it too, to fit in. Or when racists ramble on about racial purity and white supremacy and bullshit like that.

The torture mobs back then were no different. If everyone wielded torches and threw rocks at some poor woman in the town square, it felt good to be a part of the mob and throw rocks too. The same effect can be observed on social media today. If a Twitter crowd gangs up on someone, others join in and also trash the victim, even if they don't actually know the victim personally or know first hand what the victim supposedly did wrong, or if he's actually guilty or not: "A celebrity supposedly said something that could be interpreted in an offensive manner? Where is my torch?! Honey, hand me my rocks! Everyone else is throwing rocks too!"

Those museums I mentioned don't just display torture devices, but also old drawings and paintings where you can see what the people back then looked like. The crowds were laughing while throwing rocks. They were having a good time torturing one of their own. They were euphoric. And when you look at how gleeful and spiteful Twitter mobs are when they find their latest victim, you see the same joy and euphoria, thinly disguised as outrage.

MEDIEVAL DATING

Throughout history, men have treated women pretty horribly. Believe it or not, in the past even rape was considered normal and acceptable. In ancient times tribes attacked other neighboring tribes and stole their women. That was just a normal thing to do back then. And it was normal to have sex with your female slaves.

My wife and I went on a trip to Iceland recently. Incidentally, many scenes from Game of Thrones were filmed in Iceland. We visited some of the locations. Our tour guide's name was Swan. Yeah, he knows it's a dumb name, but he learned to live with it. Swan was an extra on Game of Thrones. He told us a little bit about the show and the inspiration HBO drew from the true history of his beautiful country.

At one point Swan mentioned where the first Icelandic settlers came from. He said most of the men came from Norway, while most of the women came from Ireland. Why? Because Norwegian Vikings raided and plundered Irish villages and stole their women. They kidnapped them and brought them to Iceland and made them their "wives" to be raped happily ever after. Marriage was pretty rapey back in the day. It wasn't a picnic being a *"wife"* back then. Or a *submissive*, in BDSM lingo. (Yeah, you like that idea when it's in one of your BDSM books, dontcha? You freak!)

Luckily things have changed. It's still a slow process, but at least we're making progress. Especially in the last 100 years or so. It's no longer normal to kidnap and rape women. It's no longer ok to treat women like sex objects.

Most men know that. Most men realize that women are human beings with feelings and opinions and stuff. And they're trying to do the right thing. They're not intentional douchebags. They're douchebags by accident.

RICH GUYS LIKE PRETTY YOUNG WOMEN

Tabloids are full of pictures of celebrity couples. And a lot of times you see a rich, ugly, old guy with a beautiful young wife. He wants her body. She wants his money. It's not rocket science.

It's always been like that. The big Viking chief got first dibs at the kidnapped women. Pharaohs, kings and warlords took the prettiest women for their harems. Rich, powerful men all throughout history simply took the women they wanted.

So is it any surprise that movie stars and politicians today still do the same thing?

But not all sexual predators are the same. Some sadistic fucks know that they are predators and they love every minute of it. They love to abuse their power over others and enjoy forcing themselves on a woman against her will. It makes him feel powerful. It gets him off.

As sick as that might be, it's part of human nature. As the success of Fifty Shades of Grey has shown us, there are a lot of people out there who get aroused by the thought of dominating others sexually. In BDSM, people act out their fantasies and hidden desires. But those desires have always been part of human nature, and in the past, they weren't hidden. Those desires were socially acceptable back then, so people didn't need to play-act BDSM. They simply acted on their desires, because it was the normal thing to do.

And then there are those other sexual predators. The ones who don't even know that they're predators. They were raised to treat women with respect. They know that it's not ok to objectify women. And they believe they're doing everything right. And then they get caught off guard when they get accused of sexual misconduct: "What do you mean you don't want to see my dick? How can that be?!"

THE UNINTENTIONAL PREDATOR

When plundering and pillaging fell out of fashion, and kidnap-and-rape was no longer a widespread custom to find a wife, it became perfectly normal for a rich man to woo a woman with his wealth: "Who cares if I'm old and ugly? I got bling! If you let me fuck you, you can have some of my bling."

That, in a nutshell, is how rich old men attract their hot young trophy wives. It has always been acceptable behavior, and it still is.

It happens all over the world, every single day: Young beautiful women trade sex for money in loveless relationships with ugly old rich creeps.

We might laugh when we see some sad old creep with a bad comb-over and a hot trophy wife by his side, because we know that's not love. That marriage is a sham! An abomination before the Lord! Arrest that man!!!

Just kidding. We don't arrest *that* old creep. We don't even shame him. In fact people congratulate him on the hot piece of ass he landed. And secretly they wish they had arm candy like that too.

We don't put him on trial for using economic pressure to force a woman to have sex with him. But essentially that's what he's doing. Is that not a form of sexual abuse too?

If she doesn't fulfill his sexual desires, he'll dump her and just find himself a younger, hotter trophy wife, who basically has to act as his personal sex slave if she wants to live in his mansion and get expensive clothes, jewelry and spending money from him. And the longer she stays in that arrangement, the more dependent she becomes on him and his money. She's basically prostituting herself, even if her customer is also her husband. And he's using his status and money as leverage against her, to force her to spread her legs for him.

As disgusting as that is, these loveless "marriages" are perfectly normal and perfectly acceptable in our society today. It happens every day. Nobody gets highly offended by it. Because it's called marriage, so it's ok.

So it's not really surprising when a rich old guy thinks it's acceptable to offer a woman a job in exchange for sex. Some of them honestly don't understand what's wrong with it. It's been done that way for thousands of years, and it still is done that way in Hollywood and Washington D.C. and everywhere else today. Just look at all those rich old creeps with hot young wives on TV and in the tabloids.

And when you're a rich actor or producer or politician and you see everyone around you in a "mutually beneficial relationship" with some hot young starlet, you start to assume that all women are ok with that arrangement: "Why would all these women agree to that if they weren't ok with it?"

And then you suddenly think it's a good idea to ask your secretary if she wants to see your dick. Because who wouldn't want to see your amazing dick?

These guys are not predators on purpose. They think they're doing everything right: "I asked first!"

They were told that nowadays you can't just rape a woman, no matter how rich you are. You have to ask for permission before you can fuck them. So they politely ask: "Hey, you're hot. I'm rich. Wanna fuck me? I have a lot of influence in the business and you could benefit from that." (Even if they don't say the last sentence out loud, it's implied.)

At that moment, he doesn't realize that he's not just asking the woman. He may not be choking her in a dark alley, but he still has leverage over her, and she doesn't really have much of a choice. She can say no and lose her job and never work in this business again, or she can get on her knees for him.

That is the same situation, the same sex-for-money arrangement as in all those perfectly acceptable rich-old-guy-with-hot-young-wife "marriages."

It's a sad reality that in today's society women are not judged by the content of their character, but by their looks. In high school the hot girls are the popular girls. And later in life, women who are young and hot are treated better, and seen as more valuable, than ugly or old women.

If you're a beautiful woman, everyone wants to know you, everyone wants to be your friend. Look at those Instagram girls who post half-naked selfies. They have millions of followers. If Mother Theresa was alive today, and she had an Instagram account, she'd never have as many followers as Kim Kardashian.

Meanwhile, men are not judged by their looks, but by their wallet. In our society, men are valued by how much money they have. If you're poor, you're nobody. Nobody cares what you think or what you have to say.

If you're rich, people admire you as if you were the Second Coming of Christ. Everything you say is suddenly important, simply because you're rich. People assume that you must be a better, smarter, more valuable, more important person somehow, even if you just inherited your wealth and you're as dumb as a loaf of bread.

So it's no surprise that rich men think every woman would love to have sex with them. It's the way they perceive the world. From their point of view it's true.

And they're genuinely surprised when they find out later that a woman felt like she was being forced to have sex with him. They didn't act like douchebags on purpose. They were unintentional predators.

I believe all these sex scandals will never stop until we as a society examine our values and priorities. It's not enough to shame men for behaving in a way that is deemed socially unacceptable. We need to have a national conversation about sexuality that is open and honest.

If you enjoyed this book, you'll love:

Oliver Markus Malloy

why men and women can't be friends

With candid honesty Oliver Markus Malloy explores the age-old question: "Can men and women ever really be just friends?" Women think so. But every man knows that it's impossible. Read this book and find out what really goes on in a man's mind. You will never look at opposite-sex friendships the same way again.

Lightning Source UK Ltd.
Milton Keynes UK
UKHW021247250521
384346UK00007B/1561